THE STORY OF LOUIS SHERRY

LOUIS SHERRY
The Man Whose Dreams Came True

Printing Statement:

Due to the very old age and scarcity of this book,
many of the pages may be hard to read due to the
blurring of the original text, possible missing pages,
missing text and other issues beyond our control.

Because this is such an important and rare work, we
believe it is best to reproduce this book regardless of
its original condition.

Thank you for your understanding.

THE STORY OF

Louis Sherry

AND THE BUSINESS
HE BUILT

By Edward Hungerford

NEW YORK

WILLIAM EDWIN RUDGE

1929

The Story of Louis Sherry

RAIN, splashing in the avenue outside. The cluppity-clup-clup of horses' hoofs upon the pavement blocks. The roar of trains upon the Elevated, almost directly overhead; the shriek of the whistles of their small locomotives. . . . Men and women going by, with umbrellas; the women clutching at their long skirts, to keep them clear of the glistening sidewalks. . . . Evening lights come on in the windows of the houses. And Louis Sherry stroking his moustaches as he stands in the door of his new candy shop and restaurant, which he is to open this very evening—the year is 1881.

Perhaps, he thinks, he has made a mistake in undertaking this venture. Perhaps, after all, New York is not quite ready for a place of this sort. In Paris, or in Vienna, or in London even, it might be different. But New York is hardly as large as those cities. And not nearly so sophisticated. New York is only just now beginning to be the least bit citified. It still —here at the beginnings of the "eighties"—has many of the earmarks of an overgrown town. Yet signs of a coming metropolitanism do begin to show themselves. New York already is attaining its fine new opera house, over at Broadway and Thirty-ninth Street—hardly a stone's throw from the brand-new Sherry place, in Sixth Avenue.

Already Louis Sherry is not unknown in New York. For some years past he has been employed by the fashionable Hotel Brunswick down on the north side of Madison Square. This past summer he has risen to the important post of a *maître d'hôtel,* in a smart hotel at Long Branch. . . . Long Branch has just passed through a notable season—both in a social and in a dramatic sense. First the fashionables of all the East had there assembled. There had been light and life and gayety. . . . And then, tragedy. The President of the United States, foully assassinated in the railroad station in Washington, had been brought to nearby Elberon—to linger, and then to die. . . . Not a time easily to be forgotten. And a time in which Louis Sherry walked—already a fairly conspicuous figure. Men and women of assured social position came to know him—and to like him. . . . To know him was to like him—invariably. . . . And the hour arrived when even a bowing acquaintance with the erstwhile captain of the Brunswick was, in itself, something of a social asset.

This prestige, Louis Sherry decided, in that memorable summer of 1881, to capitalize. He would set up his own business. He began to exercise actively that remarkable faculty for making friends and for holding them that was to be his, until the end of his life. He talked with the men that he had been serving—so deftly and so efficiently. He told them of his dream of immediately establishing his own enterprise. Almost to a man, they told him that they would support him in it—men like Henry Clews and F. R. Coudert and William B. Dinsmore—men whose word in New York and more than half-way around the world was like a government bond. . . . On these assurances he had leased that small building at 662 Sixth Avenue—on the south side of Thirty-eighth Street.

He took the entire building. While Sherry's first customers rarely saw other than the ground floor of what he made a confectionery shop and catering headquarters, its other stories were actively employed. In the basement he established his ice cream and pastry shops and a main kitchen. The third and fourth floors were confectionery kitchens. On the second he had his living quarters.

This then the Sherry's of beginning days—back there in the autumn of 1881. . . . Not many evenings to be standing in the doorway of his shop, watching the traffic in the avenue. Louis Sherry's friends are keeping their good faith with him. Business begins to pour in upon him. The new enterprise differs from many others, before and since, in that, from the outset it is a pronounced success.

One year, two years, three years pass. . . . And all the while business continues to increase. The basement of the adjoining market is leased and occupied by the widely expanding catering arm. . . . . . Then comes the not-soon-to-be-forgotten Kirmess in the dazzling new Metropolitan Opera House. Two solid days of it. On each of them, Louis Sherry is to serve to the multitude, a lunch, a table d'hôte dinner, a late supper. This is his first enterprise on such a very large scale. . . . And the next day the newspapers are recording it all as a huge success.

Now the orders come fairly pouring in upon the head of New York's newest important restaurateur—this charming man of French ancestry and French manners, yet who, it develops, actually was born in St. Albans, Vermont. Bishop Potter gives a luncheon of four hundred covers, a churchly

affair, and Louis Sherry adds another laurel to his crown.
. . . On the last evening of September, 1885, he captures
the Badminton Assembly. . . . Still another laurel.

The yellowed pages of his old order-book, still carefully
preserved, tell the story, simply but unmistakably. . . . Mrs.
Paran Stevens will have a dinner for seven at her austere but
beautiful house in the lower Fifth Avenue. Sherry serves.
. . . Herman Oelrichs seeks to give a "different" sort of a
party. He has it; on the new tug, *Rob 2*. It is an overwhelm-
ing success. Sherry serves. . . . The Rockaway Hunt—
always a smart affair. Sherry serves. . . . The Mendels-
sohn Glee Club, Kaffee Klatsche, with café frappé actually
as its dominating feature. A triumph. Sherry serves. . . .
Finally that huge affair of April 13, 1887, at the Columbia
College that still stood in Madison Avenue, at Forty-ninth
Street. *Two thousand* hungry folk served by Louis Sherry,
and a faintly penciled memorandum records the fact that
fifty gallons of lemonade and claret punch will be needed.
The good old days!

The old order-book speaks eloquently of the Elegant
Eighties and the Gay Nineties; of the delightful New York
that was and that never can come again—at least, not again

in exactly the same way. The names of that New York crowd upon its pages . . . Mrs. Nicholas Fish . . . Fahnestock . . . De Peyster . . . William C. Whitney (affairs in his town house up at Sixty-seventh Street and at the rambling country place at Westbury, out on the Island) . . . Rhinelander (the annual Christmas dinner up at the Forty-eighth Street house) . . . Roosevelt . . . Hoyt . . . Wendell . . . Mrs. Henry Villard. . . . Always it is, "Sherry serves."

How quickly he becomes a real New York institution, widespread, all-embracing! Dewitt Flanagan, the brewer, uses him for his wondrous affairs. So does the exquisite Elsie de Wolfe. That rare littérateur, Charles Scribner. . . . That man whom all New York knows, Doctor H. M. Biggs. . . . The genial Peter Fenelon Collier gives a breakfast at 7 o'clock in the morning—at Sherry's. They come, before dawn of a December day, and they have bouillon and oyster patties and cutlets and canvas-back duck, lobster salad, an aspic galantine, ices and cake and call it a perfect breakfast—at 7 o'clock in the morning. New York also lived—in those days.

"From the start I determined not to let anything go out of my house that was not made in the best possible way and out of the best and most expensive materials on the market,"

Louis Sherry once said, speaking in a reminiscent vein of his beginnings in the restaurant business. He could have told nothing truer of himself. It used to be said in New York that Sherry would pay little or no attention to complaints of the prices that he charged; but that the slightest criticism of the quality of anything that he served or the method of its service set him at once on edge and seeking to rectify matters. This early became a cardinal principle of the Sherry institution—one of the firm rocks upon which the entire enterprise was securely built.

At that time Sherry went on to say that he had set the long-established New York house of Delmonico as a standard that he must reach—and, if possible, excel. He realized that this was no small ambition.

"I was much disappointed at first," he continued, "because some of the people down at the seashore (he was referring to his experience that summer at Long Branch) who had so glibly promised to patronize me if I went into business for myself, still gave their orders to Delmonico and to Pinard. But, I reflected, this was only natural. Delmonico and Pinard were tried and proved, and I was but an experiment."

So had Louis Sherry first embarked upon the craft of his making.

Studiously he sought to discover the real wishes of the high type of patrons that he desired. (Here was another cardinal principle of the budding institution.) At that time, table decorations, light and graceful and unusual, were in especial vogue. He featured these. Over in Broadway, the newest Gilbert and Sullivan operetta, *The Mikado,* was scoring a tremendous hit. Sherry cornered the New York market in Japanese parasols. . . . Of these he made most effective use. . . . Fresh orders poured in upon him. . . . He went overseas and made a study of the way that all these things were being done over there. . . . When he returned his business had increased to a point that made a step to Fifth Avenue—just then being invaded by trade for the first time —an imminent necessity. Yet, for some time he debated in his own mind the wisdom of this step. . . . The man who had stood in the doorway of his first shop, there in Sixth Avenue, and had heard the horses' hoofs go cluppity-clup-clup in the rain was still a little dubious—although hopeful —of the future.

Yet within another two decades that future was to seem

really assured. . . . The Elegant Eighties went out and the Gay Nineties came tripping in. . . . New York grew, and so grew its ideas of truly elegant entertainment. Louis Sherry plunged in and moved his establishment over to Fifth Avenue at the corner of Thirty-seventh Street—in what had been one of the fine old residences of the town. It was the property of the Goelet family who remodeled it for its new purposes; installing both a large and a small ball-room, a small restaurant—a rather new feature of the business but one that was to grow rapidly in favor—and the confectionery shop. This new establishment opened in 1890. After which the doors of the Sixth Avenue shop were closed, forever.

New names now began to appear on Sherry's books. Among them, those of E. D. Morgan, of Hempstead, and of George F. Schieffelin. . . . The ramifications of Sherry's work widened, greatly. George J. Baldwin, away down at Savannah, Georgia, gave a magnificent entertainment in January, 1890—three hundred guests present. Nothing less than Louis Sherry would possibly do for him. So Louis Sherry went down to that old Southern city—in a special Pullman and two baggage-cars. His men carried the china, the linen, the decorations, the food and the drink in these last. As the train rolled southward and crossed into Georgia, Sherry's chefs already were beginning the preparation of the dinner.

Eventually — almost inevitably — the Thirty-seventh Street place became in turn too small. New York was all the while moving uptown; irresistibly and no longer slowly. Sherry felt impelled to join the tide. He decided that, for a time at least, the corner of Fifth Avenue and Forty-fourth Street would be close to, if not the exact center of the social life of the town. Accordingly, he selected a large site at the southwest corner of those two thoroughfares and there it was that he caused to be erected, the handsome twelve-story building that was entirely given over to his restaurant, his catering establishment and the suites of living apartments operated in connection with them.

Here was a real restaurant!

In all its days—and New York no longer was young— the town had seen nothing to be even compared with it. Without, a structure of remarkable solidity and dignity (today, converted to bank and office purposes, it holds its own among the handsome buildings of a truly magnificent world thoroughfare); within, it was a place of moving beauty, of exquisite appeal. A·large restaurant for ladies and gentlemen occupied the Fifth Avenue street frontage; and back of that, on Forty-fourth Street, was the men's grill that speedily became popular as a lunching place with the business men who, even then, were beginning to multiply in the neighborhood. At night, "downtown" came uptown; the grill became a remarkably popular rendezvous for dinners, both formal and informal. The front restaurant held, at almost all hours, its distinctly formal character. . . . Upstairs there was a splendid ballroom, many lesser rooms, for private entertaining of every sort. And above these the living quarters of many distinguished New Yorkers.

Frank A. Munsey came to live in the Forty-fourth Street Sherry's the very day that it was opened—October 10, 1898 —and stayed until it closed its doors—in 1919. He occupied a suite of twenty-seven rooms. . . . Another huge group of living apartments was assigned to the officers of the United Gas Improvement Company, for their frequent trips over from Philadelphia. This presently became known as the "U. G. I. Suite."

All New York found its way to the new Sherry's. One of

its most steady customers was the late J. Pierpont Morgan. He liked Louis Sherry and he liked the unusual restaurant that Louis Sherry conducted, and when he was in New York he came to it nearly every afternoon. The employees about the place came to speak of him as "Uncle John."

By this time there was no mistaking the prestige of Sherry's.

If ever there had been the slightest doubt, whatsoever, about it, it all went sailing to the four winds when Mrs. Astor bestowed her regal favor upon the place, by giving a great ball underneath its roof. After which all New York came, unreservedly. One saw there unquestioned social leaders, such as Mrs. Astor—high captains of finance, such as Mr. Morgan—undisputed leaders in literature, such as Richard Harding Davis; great stars of the stage, such as the popular Ethel Barrymore and her beloved uncle, the late John Drew. . . . This list might easily be extended—and indefinitely.

When Louis Sherry first built his great restaurant there in Fifth Avenue at the Forty-fourth Street corner, there was little else roundabout but the fine old houses of oldtime New Yorkers. While on the block of the Avenue that immediately faced his establishment was the huge Synagogue (recently torn down), a stable of the New York Cab Company, and a quaint succession of two-storied wooden edifices— one of them Tyson's Market and another, the Willow Tree Saloon, confronted by a faded and almost lifeless tree, which still had the audacity to stretch its few withered branches out at the curb edge of the Avenue. . . . Fifth Avenue was then in a curious transition. . . . Above the new restaurant many more fine residences crowded together, but within a few months after Sherry's first opened its doors they were beginning to tear down some of these; at the northwest corner of Fifth Avenue and Forty-fourth Street, diagonally across the way. Here it was that presently they began to build a new Delmonico's, for the final step of that historic house, this time north from Twenty-sixth Street. . . . Delmonico's— the only restaurant that Louis Sherry ever really recognized as a rival—took its position upon that opposite corner in 1899, and there for twenty glorious years New York's two great capitals of good food and good service existed, in a neighborly and friendly competition.

Despite the great development of the restaurant service after the opening at Forty-fourth Street, there was no diminution in the catering function of Louis Sherry's business.

On the contrary, it grew—hugely. Both in New York, and out. Going to a place as far off as Savannah, ceased to be an event in its history. Chicago, Pittsburgh, Washington—all became portions of Sherry's field. And finally San Francisco.

A decade or more ago, the great triennial convocation of the Protestant Episcopal Church was held in the city by the Golden Gate. One of the most distinguished attendants at these affairs was Mr. J. Pierpont Morgan. Mr. Morgan had an aversion to the publicity of the average American hotel. Moreover, he wished to entertain in a rather large fashion at the convention. So he spoke to Louis Sherry. A full month before the opening of the great convocation, Sherry agents boarded a train for San Francisco. Twenty men were picked from the New York staff. A fine old San Francisco residence was hired. When he first saw it, Sherry's manager, in charge of the group, sensed that the rare, antiquated furnishings of the old house would not suit Mr. Morgan's critical taste. Accordingly, they were all torn out and replaced; the entire building, from cellar to attic, transformed. Before the New York banker and his party of clerical guests arrived, the establishment was in as perfect running order as a well-managed club which has been functioning for years past. . . .

Three days after the group of churchmen departed for the East, the house was completely dismantled. The men who had been operating it were on a train home-bound. . . . Sherry served.

A great deal lies in the full interpretation of such a phrase. . . . There came a time, not long after, when a certain New Yorker decided to honor an important social occasion upstate with a gift of a large and most wonderful cake. Sherry's got the order. As sometimes happens, it got it at the eleventh hour. That was the hour at least when that same manager of the New York establishment, arriving at his office, found the huge cake still unfinished; with the order imperative that it go to the state capital on the one o'clock train out of the nearby Grand Central Terminal . . . . There was a deal of confusion. And some excuse for it:

The favors—thirty lovely gold bracelets that were to have been imbedded deep within the cake—had not yet arrived. The masterpiece could not be completed until they had been inserted. "Finish baking that cake," ordered the manager, "but do not put on the decorations."

Then he set out in a taxi to get the favors. He found them at the shipping-room of the jeweler's, took them with him to the station, and there, by appointment, met two of the chef's crew. A drawing-room in a Pullman had been engaged. In it, between New York and Albany, the cake was finished. Slits were cut down into it, the bracelets were inserted and the candles and the icing were fitted as the swift train made its way. It was ready and on time. . . . "Never disappoint a patron," was an early tradition of Louis Sherry. "Get a special train, a special boat—anything—but never disappoint a patron."

Apparently, more than a mere phrase, that tradition! Not merely a tradition, but a fixed policy—a part of the Sherry creed, if you please. The third cardinal principle, if you would so put it.

Twenty glorious years there at Forty-fourth Street. Times far too good to last for ever.

In the modern New York, twenty years is a very long time indeed. Times change quickly in the great city of the Americas.

Twenty glorious years. . . . The World War came—and went. Unforgettable parades passed up the Avenue in front of Sherry's, and men and women in the uniforms of all the Allies filled his restaurants. . . . Times were changing—swiftly. . . . New York still kept surging uptown. There were few private residences left around Sherry's any more. Business was indeed coming in; with a mighty swing. On every side office-buildings were uprising. Fifth Avenue, south of Fifty-ninth Street had ceased—forever—to be a residential street, and so had many of the side byways that lead off from it. The pressure of land values in that section became terrific. From it, Sherry's was by no means immune.

Then came prohibition—that deadening statute that made good lunching and good dining and good supping so very, very difficult indeed—and then, the thing almost undreamed of—Sherry's closed its doors at Forty-fourth Street; there in the very height of its prosperity. The thing was unthinkable. And yet the thing was done—on a May evening in 1919.

So it was to be written in the annals of New York social life, that Sherry's impeccable Forty-fourth Street place closed its doors after dinner on the evening of May 17, 1919. . . . There had been a good deal of dash about its opening twenty-one years earlier—an inspection by the press and a formal reception and dinner to many distinguished and representative New Yorkers. . . . The closing was a simple matter.

A sharp contrast. It came after the last dinner had been served, the last check paid, the last waiter tipped. . . . Lights went out, the key was turned in the great outer doors, for the first time in history at any early hour. . . . A few days later, the wreckers were tearing out the fine fittings of the place. The huge Lille and Beauvais tapestries—they are said to be valued at more than $200,000—were sent down to the Waldorf-Astoria. . . . A little later the Guarantee Trust Company, the new owner of the building, was setting up its most important uptown branch on the ground floor of what had been the capital of good living; the upper floors were being transformed into offices. . . . And Louis Sherry was on his way to Europe, to enjoy a long-anticipated and a well-earned rest.

But Sherry's itself did not cease to exist. Sherry's could not die. It even could not be permitted to live merely as a wraith, or a pleasant memory of the New York of yester-year. Its spark of life was, seemingly, inextinguishable. And presently it blazed forth again—in new light and new luster.

As the doors of the famous Forty-fourth Street house closed, those of a new Sherry's, much further uptown—this time on Fifth Avenue at Fifty-eighth Street—were opening.

This last was not to be known as a restaurant. It was, in chief measure, a confectionery store.

One of the very notable successes that Louis Sherry long ago had builded for himself was in the making of sweetmeats—of a distinctive and superior sort. Without advertising or particular exploitation of any kind, these had come into increasing favor. The cardinal principles of the Sherry credo—chief of them all the endless striving for quality of the finest sort—which expressed themselves in Sherry's confections were firmly established and that tongue-lingering phrase "when it's a matter of good taste—Sherry's," was born.

Yet the Fifty-eighth Street house was not entirely limited to the large and steadily expanding vending of confections. It also specialized in light luncheon, afternoon tea, and the like. And it provided a most central and convenient headquarters for the catering function of the establishment.

The announcement of the contemplated closing of the Forty-fourth Street restaurant had sent shivers of apprehension up and down the well-poised backbones of smart New York matrons. They wrote and they telephoned in protest. What was going to happen to the catering end of the business! There must be enough good waiters still left in the Sherry organization to maintain the catering service; as well as the confectionery shop.

There were.

Thus it was that the unquenchable flame of Sherry life was not extinguished. After Forty-fourth Street had shut, the enterprise still went forward, although for a season in a somewhat diminished form. After all, there *were* enough good waiters left in New York—good personnel of every sort—to maintain in the Sherry catering service the high standards set by its founder. And it was precisely that service that continued to keep Sherry's alive—in that handsome shop on the ground floor at the corner of Fifth Avenue and Fifty-eighth Street.

In great New York, institutions come quickly—go even more quickly. Times change. And so do fashions. What is up today is down tomorrow. And sometimes—not often— the reverse.

No one in the first decade of the present century could have easily imagined that Fifth Avenue—New York's superb *place des dames;* the Fifth Avenue that was, and still is, one of the most magnificent streets in all the world—

could be equalled and, perhaps, even surpassed by a rival thoroughfare.

Yet precisely this thing came to pass.

A parallel street that formerly had held but little dignity, little beauty for itself—largely because of a railroad and a railroad yard that occupied its very heart—suddenly emerged into a thoroughfare of great brilliancy and of great beauty—with an evenness and symmetry of architectural adornment such as Fifth Avenue in all its days, never had boasted.

Aladdin came, rubbed a magic wand and the new Park Avenue came into being.

Perhaps you know the story yourself.

How the New York Central Railroad suddenly decided to change the method of propulsion of its many, many through and suburban passenger trains that each day enter the Grand Central Terminal, from steam to electricity. How the New Haven road, which for many years past has been its co-tenant in the Grand Central, simultaneously decided upon the selfsame step. How some inventor, with the heaven-sent dream of an idealist, suggested that with this radical change in motive power, the black and ugly and smoke-

THREE HUNDRED PARK AVENUE
Good Manners Finding Architectural Expression

filled railroad yard that for years past had been an eyesore in the heart of Manhattan be banished forever and a new heart created for the big town—a heart that for orderly planning and cleanliness and sheer articulate beauty should not be beaten—or even equalled—the whole world over. For not Rome, nor Vienna, not even Paris, may rival New York structurally, when New York makes up her mind to do a huge thing—and do it well.

So went the old Grand Central and its dirty, black-breasted yard. So came the new Grand Central—a splendid great railroad station—and so came the new Park Avenue—smart motor-cars and taxis and well-dressed folk afoot where once dingy switch-engines had wheezed and chortled and switchmen were forever running alongside the shiny tracks. . . . And with the new Park Avenue came many other new things—apartments and office buildings, a new St. Bartholomew's Church and last, but not least, the new Sherry's.

Three Hundred Park Avenue!

To the seasoned New Yorker, here is an address with which to conjure.

To his mind it summons an instant picture of social dis-

tinction—exclusiveness, dignity, yet a certain sort of gra-
ciousness withal. The good manners that ever are the heri-
tage of good breeding. Good manners and good breeding
finding architectural expression, of an unmistakable sort.

Such is the Sherry's at Three Hundred Park Avenue.

In the main the new establishment followed the general
character of the old—at Forty-fourth Street on the neighbor-
ing avenue. A large formal restaurant on the ground floor
and a small informal one on the same floor were supple-
mented by ballrooms and their necessary accessories on the
next floor above. After which came fourteen stories of living
apartments—individual homes, in the fullest sense of the
word. There were ninety of these, the most of them ranging
in size from a parlor, bedroom and bath to five bedrooms
(with baths), library, salon, drawing-room, butler's pantry,
kitchen and servants' quarters. In a number of instances
multiples of these last units were taken. One New York man
of recognized wealth and position leased nearly an entire
floor of them—for his exclusive use.

To open this superb new establishment, Louis Sherry returned from overseas in 1922. He conferred with its finan-
cial supporters—General T. Coleman du Pont, Colonel

Benjamin McAlpin, Lewis L. Dunham, Lucius M. Boomer, Percy Rockefeller and Thomas Cochran prominent amongst them.

To this new Park Avenue Sherry's, Louis Sherry himself gave the keenest personal interest and attention. As Chairman of the Board of the company, he attended the opening of the new establishment and renewed old friendships once again among both patrons and employees. There were many of both—none forgotten. . . . A little later Louis Sherry again retired from active business, although his official connection with it did not cease. His years thereafter were few. He was no longer in the best of health. . . . And when his death was announced, June 9, 1926, that little segment of New York that had known him intimately and well, professed no large astonishment. And showed no little real grief.

Real institutions many times long outlive the men who gave them birth. The old order had passed, Louis Sherry was in his grave, but the real institution that was to live and to be his real monument through the years only increased in strength and prestige. New York clung to it. . . . The new restaurant ranked with the old in the distinction of its patronage. It still so ranks. To state the names of its present-day

patrons might be an offense to good taste. It is quite enough
to say that they are legion. A legion whose tastes and fancies
often vary. Vary even in the favor given this room—or that.
Now it is the great main room of the Sherry restaurant—
with those wonderful tapestries again hanging on its walls
—that has the largest favor—and now it is the stately foyer
—the little tea shop at the Fifty-first Street corner that has its
special devotees. . . . But it all is Sherry's.

This Park Avenue Sherry's today is over-topped, liter-
ally, by a newer and far taller member of the family; which
raises its stately head at the northeast corner of Fifth Avenue
and Fifty-ninth Street, the site of the former Netherland
Hotel, from which it takes its distinctive title of the Sherry-
Netherland.

Of a truth, it has been said that this structure, dominating
the New York sky line in its vicinity, is, indeed, the last word
in modern living. Thirty-nine stories in height, it reaches
higher into the sky than any other residence apartment building has ever before reached. Yet this is not all: In all the
world there is no more beautifully situated apartment building than this. Central Park is its front lawn and demesne.
Northward and westward the restful greens of its eight

LIKE A MEDIAEVAL CASTLE
Rises the Tall Tower of the new Sherry-Netherland

hundred acres of foliage charm the vision and rest the eye; through three-quarters of the year; the remainder of the twelve months there are apt to be visions of snowy whiteness—upon occasion trees ice-incrusted and crystallized in the morning scene, to an almost unthinkable beauty.

As Three Hundred Park Avenue, in 1922, the newest Sherry's stood—and still stands—in a center of the finest social life of New York, so does the still newer Sherry-Netherland command another vantage-point in the social existence of Manhattan. In it, the same excellent scheme of living, already so well-developed at Three Hundred Park Avenue, is once more firmly established. It is this feature of the establishment that ranks in attractiveness with its architectural distinction and its rare location.

Three Hundred Park Avenue paved the way for what was practically "a new way of living" in New York. It combined many of the best features of modern hotel life with those of modern apartment house life. In other words, the Sherry-Netherland and Three Hundred Park Avenue combine the great freedom of living in the modern New York hotel—the utter freedom from care as to the procuring of food and other supplies, the hiring and supervision of servants and the like—with the best features of modern apartment house life—seclusion and privacy, chief of all of these.

. . . As a hotel, providing for transient as well as resident guests, there are, in the Sherry-Netherland, two restaurants. These, properly quiet and somewhat secluded, are conducted by Sherry's; in the impeccable Sherry way.

In the Sherry-Netherland, Sherry catering becomes, however, not a matter of a single meal or a group of meals but a feature as consistent as a resident of the establishment cares to make it. Always the cuisine is ready and awaiting orders. Night and day it is at the service of the man or woman who makes his or her home in these houses. And always it is the distinctive service, upbuilded, for ever and a day, on the cardinal principles that Louis Sherry himself set down.

Never is there forgotten the fact that the Sherry-Netherland is designed to be the home of quiet and refined folk, to whom living means always a delicate combination of comfort and of dignity. Many of the residents of the building maintain an apartment within it as but one of two or more permanent homes. . . . The keeping of a private house in New York has become such a difficult matter that these far-sighted folk prefer to arrive in town, turn a key in a lock and

THE NEWEST SHERRY'S
Just Completed at Madison Avenue and Sixty-second Street

find every comfort and other facility that they have in their other homes ready and waiting them.

This means, of course, trained service—of every sort and variety—in addition to that of merely providing food and drink. It means constant attendance, unfailing forethought and good taste, but these things so long since became marked standards of Sherry organization, that they need no extended comment here.

Sherry's grows. It seeks, for the convenience of its patrons, to place itself in touch at every possible point where there is largest need for its services. This being so, there was opened a Sherry shop—in almost every respect similar to the first one on Fifth Avenue and Fifty-eighth Street—further down the Avenue at Thirty-fifth Street. This meets the luncheon and tea necessities of downtown shoppers, supplies a convenient fountain service, and the confectionery requirements of this shopping neighborhood.

Of a distinctly different sort is the newest Sherry shop just opened at Madison Avenue and Sixty-second Street. In an impressive two-storied building—designed for it in the modern mode, with great simplicity and charm—Sherry's dispenses rare table delicacies of every sort. Confections, of course. The Sherry coffee. But far more. Viands ordinarily hard to obtain, but greatly appreciated by hostesses, are sold. Such, for instance, as caviar and olive oil of rare quality, pâté de foie gras, French vegetables and conserves of many sorts. These are the things that hitherto only stewards of high grade hotels, restaurants and clubs, have been able ordinarily to locate—at their very best. Many hostesses have longed for them but have not known where to obtain them. The Sherry Table Delicacies establishment at Madison Avenue and Sixty-second Street fills this genuine and essential social need. . . . These delectable things, heretofore available at Sherry's through his restaurant and catering service, can now be "sent home" as may be desired. And "home" in this instance, may be translated not only any point upon the Continent, but to almost any point in all creation, where good living is really enjoyed.

In no other way, perhaps, has Sherry's gained greater favor in later years than in its remarkable development of its business in confections. It has dropped the old-fashioned word "candy" forever from its vocabulary. "Candy" does not quite suit the Sherry type of sweetmeat. "Candy" is all right in its way, but not in the Sherry way. "Confections" is the word that best suits its super-sweetmeats. . . . Sherry's confections made in a remarkably bright and clean modern structure in Long Island City—are carrying the hallmark of the highest in New York catering, not merely to the far corners of America but overseas as well. A distinctive feature of the distribution of these confections is in steamer presents. The unusual and really beautiful lavender boxes of Sherry's occupy many of the staterooms of the smartest liners that each week go out from the port of New York.

The steadily increasing vogue of Sherry's confections now is being rivalled by another specialty of the house—Sherry's coffee—a blend of rare degree. This has leaped into tremendous popularity. On both sides of the Atlantic. Perhaps, if anything, even more so on the European side than on the American. The Yankee in France develops almost as avid a thirst for home brew coffee, with sweet cream, as for the "wines of the land." . . . Just after the war Sherry opened one of its typical shops in Paris in the Rue de Castiglione—cheek by jowl with the Hotel Meurice. This shop swept into immediate favor. At last, it was said, one could get real American coffee—in the heart of the old French capital. . . . And there were so many Americans that wanted their own sort of coffee, to say nothing of the candies and other sweets and confections to which their tastes were long since attuned and that their very hearts desired that presently the original Paris Sherry's was almost overburdened by its popularity. So eyes were cast about for another location. That has just been achieved. A new Sherry's was opened this last year—at the Rond Point, in the Champs Elysées and in a section of Paris into which smart retail trade is now coming, by leaps and by bounds. New York is not the only city that grows swiftly. . . . In the meantime the Rue de Castiglione shop remains open—and still is immensely popular. Two blades of grass have been made to grow where but one grew before.

Back of all these well-located and most convenient Sherry establishments is always that other, unseen but very real, Sherry's that reaches its fingers all through New York and for many miles outside of New York—the catering Sherry's.

This is the Sherry's that comes to you and says:

"Madam, you may give your servants an evening off on the day of your party. We will do it *all*."

Sherry means this. Of course, if there is a butler—perhaps an oldtime family appendage who is as much a part of

IN PARIS, TOO, SHERRY'S
*A View from the New Establishment Looking
Across the Rond Point*

the house as the broad front door—Sherry's can and will use him. Sherry's is adjustable. Sherry's is pliable. If it were not so, it could not go about the country giving parties of every sort—receptions, weddings, dances, dinners—all the rest of it. Similarly, if the hostess has her own preferences in music, Sherry's again bows to her wishes. That is part of Sherry's service.

On the other hand, all that Sherry's asks is the hostess' kitchen, bared, if you please, of all its working appendages. The necessary details will be arranged as soon as the day, the hour, the character and the size of the entertainment have been fixed by the hostess. . . . Next comes the menu. It must be varied. It must be alluring. If possible, a bit exotic as to its character. But, above all things, it must be well-balanced. The days when the parties of New York society were mere gorges of food and drink are past. Nowadays, the subtle power of the dietitian shows itself.

Of course, the factor of transport from Sherry's kitchens to the hostess' home comes into the reckoning, but this is Sherry's worry, not hers. She never even hears of it. Never knows of the movement of a whole fleet of motor-trucks, of the marshalling of a regiment of containers—of metal and of pottery, each designed to keep its contents (hot or cold) at a fairly even temperature—which permit of a wide range of food selection.

Here is about the way that the thing is done:

Let us assume that a woman of social position has definitely decided to have a dinner-dance at her home in upper Park Avenue, on a certain evening. Late in the afternoon the Sherry's Army of Good Things begins to arrive. There is a complete kitchen staff and a corps of waiters, including a head-waiter. There are pantrymen and pantrywomen—behind the scenes, and in front of them, neat maids for the cloak rooms and men to be stationed at the front door and out at the curb. As the canopy springs up and the red carpet goes down, a carriage call device also shows itself and, at just the right hour, a traffic policeman, especially assigned for the evening, makes his appearance. Sherry's has arranged all of these. So has Sherry's provided the "bridge-room," including not only the chairs and the tables, but the score pads. All the minor paraphernalia for almost any conceivable sort of private entertainment is carried as a part of the Sherry equipment. As much of the cookery as is possible is performed, of course, in Sherry's own kitchens. Reverting to an engineer's phrase, it is "assembled" at the house of the entertainment. Yet the list of culinary possibilities is almost infinite. . . . The coming of the dawn sees the army moving out once again. The motor trucks appear at the curb. Into them go the delightfully dissipated-looking empty containers, the tables, the chairs, the bridge score pads, the door awning—all the rest of it. It is all put away with the cleanly orderliness of a departing circus. There really is no better simile of efficient prearrangement and plan. Before morning Sherry's is out of the house. The home servants at their posts once more. A large event has been accomplished and with an astonishingly small amount of trouble.

Here, in a few brief pages, is the record of Sherry's—the Sherry's of yesterday and of today. Back of this outer structure of a completely functioning and most sizable New York institution, is the unseen but very real fabric that Louis Sherry himself created. The creation of an utterly unusual man. Like all men who found successful enterprises, Louis Sherry builded, not upon impulse or haphazard guess, but always upon firm principles. These have been set down already; his determination to have the best in quality, both in materials and in men; his careful, tireless studying of the real wishes of his patrons; his quick adaptability to emergency; the eternal vigilance and supervision that keeps an organization functioning at its very best. These cardinal principles remain the foundation stones of the business. Together, they are, and will continue to be, the real meaning of the hallmark "Sherry's." The phrase "when it's a matter of good taste—Sherry's" is, after all, but a phrase. The principles behind it, alone make it more than a mere grouping of words; make it a promise forever to be faced, and to be fulfilled—to the letter.

This record of a real institution of the New York of yesterday and of the New York of today might be continued indefinitely. But enough has been written to show how Sherry's has grown in prestige and strength and, yes, in the affections of New Yorkers, through forty-eight years of existence, and how it continues to expand with each new demand of the social day. It will continue to grow and thrive because like all institutions really worth-while it is founded on high principles—the principles laid down by the man who started it and whose name it bears—Louis Sherry.